St. Patrick's Day

Dorothy Goeller

Bailey Books
an imprint of
Enslow Publishers, Inc.
40 Industrial Road
Box 398
Berkeley Heights, NJ 07922
USA
http://www.enslow.com

Bailey Books, an imprint of Enslow Publishers, Inc.

Library of Congress Cataloging-in-Publication Data

Goeller, Dorothy.
St. Patrick's day / Dorothy Goeller.
p. cm. — (All about holidays)
Includes index.
Summary: "Simple text and photographs present a story with a St. Patrick's Day theme"—Provided by publisher.
ISBN 978-0-7660-3808-0
1. Saint Patrick's Day—Juvenile literature. I. Title. II. Title: Saint Patrick's Day.
GT4995.P3G64 2011
394.262—dc22 2010013466
Paperback ISBN: 978-1-59845-177-1

Printed in the United States of America

062010 Lake Book Manufacturing, Inc., Melrose Park, IL

10 9 8 7 6 5 4 3 2 1

To Our Readers: We have done our best to make sure all Internet Addresses in this book were active and appropriate when we went to press. However, the author and the publisher have no control over and assume no liability for the material available on those Internet sites or on other Web sites they may link to. Any comments or suggestions can be sent by e-mail to comments@enslow.com or to the address on the back cover.

Enslow Publishers, Inc., is committed to printing our books on recycled paper. The paper in every book contains 10% to 30% post-consumer waste (PCW). The cover board on the outside of each book contains 100% PCW. Our goal is to do our part to help young people and the environment too!

Photo Credits: Shutterstock.com

Cover Photo: Shutterstock.com

Note to Parents and Teachers

Help pre-readers get a jumpstart on reading. These lively stories introduce simple concepts with repetition of words and short simple sentences. Photos and illustrations fill the pages with color and effectively enhance the text. Free Educator Guides are available for this series at www.enslow.com. Search for the *All About Holidays* series name.

Contents

Words to Know

down

green

up

I see green all around me.

432
1933
SAINT PATRICK

Green up!

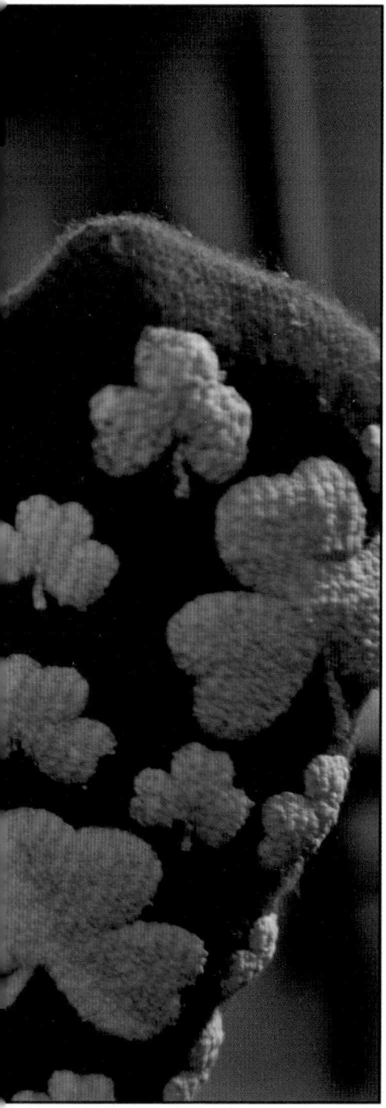

Green down!

SOLD BY
CAFE

Green all around the town!

Green up!

Green down!

Green all around the town!

Green up!

On
St. Patrick's
Day
I'm Irish...

Green down!

HAPPY
St. Patricks
DAY

Oh, I know why I see green all around!

It's St. Patrick's Day!

Read More

Haugen, Brenda. *St. Patrick's Day.* Minneapolis, Minn.: Picture Window Books, 2004.

Holub, Joan. *Good Luck!: A St. Patrick's Day Story.* New York: Aladdin Paperbacks, 2007.

Web Sites

Family Fun. *St. Patrick's Day Kids Ideas.* <familyfun.go.com/st-patricks-day>

10 Ways to Celebrate—ParentDish. *St. Patrick's Day for Kids.* <www.parentdish.com/2010/03/15/st-patricks-day-for-kids-10-ways-to-celebrate/>

Index

Guided Reading Level: B

Guided Reading Leveling System is based on the guidelines recommended by Fountas and Pinnell.

Word Count: 41